The Expert's Guide to

TEENAGERS

10 Interviews with Professionals Who Share What They've Learned

Bill Abbott

Apr. 2016

The Expert's Guide to

TEENAGERS

10 Interviews with Professionals Who Share What They've Learned

Bill Corbett

AUTHOR OF THE AWARD-WINNING PARENTING BOOK, *LOVE, LIMITS, & LESSONS*

The Expert's Guide to TEENAGERS

Cooperative Kids Publishing
Post Office Box 432
Enfield, CT 06083-432
info@CooperativeKids.com

Printed in the United States of America
ISBN: 978-0-9821121-6-8

Learn more information at:
www.BillCorbett.com

Table of Contents

Introduction

I bet you have questions about your kids. If you don't, then I'd like to interview you because you are an exception to the rule. When I first had children, I only knew one thing for sure—I wanted to be a good father to my children. I had a lot of questions and it was hard knowing what to do because I hadn't learned as much as I would have liked from my own experience as a child.

To become a better parent, I spent years researching and reading. When I talked to other parents I realized how many of them were struggling with raising their kids too, and decided to become a parent educator so I could start sharing what I'd learned with a larger audience.

Later I returned to school and got a degree in clinical psychology so I could converse, discuss, and share information with my peers. I started offering parent education classes and also began producing my own TV show - *Creating Cooperative Kids,* so I could reach a larger audience.

We all need help when it comes to being better parents. There isn't a manual and we can't always rely on instinct. Every child is unique; every parent is unique; every situation is unique. What most of us really need is a place to start. One good idea, one insight, one technique is sometimes all we need to get on the right track. That was the intention of my TV show and my parenting classes, and that's my intention with this book—to give you a place to start, or to continue, your journey of becoming the parent you'd like to be.

The interviews in this book were originally segments of my TV show. A lot of people have found them on their local cable providers, or on the internet, but I wanted to make sure that readers had access to them too. So I had the interviews transcribed and have compiled them into a series of books.

Each expert represented in this book feels the same way I do and wanted to share their knowledge and wisdom with you too. We all know your struggles. We all want to help.

This book is the first book in a series of expert guides compiled just for you.

DISCLAIMER: This book is an educational and informational resource and is not intended to be a substitute for family counseling or psychotherapy. Because the interviews are transcriptions of previously recorded interviews, portions may have been edited to ensure that they accurately relay the information intended, and to improve readability.

A special thank you to my talented editor Valerie Utton for giving me the idea to create this book series, and for her professional content editing skills that polished it up for print.

Bill Corbett

Interview 1:
Why Teens Behave the Way They Do

Bill: Many parents of teens have probably thought once or twice about selling their teenager to the zoo! Teens seem to act strange, they wear strange clothes, they lie, they tell secrets, and they become very argumentative at times. Sometimes it feels like an alien creature has inhabited the body of our once sweet and fun loving child. In this interview, you're going to find out exactly what is going on with today's modern teen with the help of my guest, Dr. Anthony Wolf, a practicing clinical psychologist who has worked with adolescents for over 30 years. He is the author of one of my favorite books on teens,

Get Out Of My Life: But first can you drive me and Cheryl to the mall.

Dr. Wolf, I can't tell you how many times I've heard that type of phrase, or variations of it, while raising my own three children and three stepchildren. I'd like for you to help us understand what's going on with these kids. We know that some sort of transition takes place anywhere between the ages of 9 and 13, and it seems as if their whole demeanor, and sometimes their behavior, changes. I think a lot of parents see their child at the age of 13, just as if they were 7 and expecting to see the same behaviors. I think with your help, we can give parents somewhat of a foundation of knowledge about their teens that will help them make smart decisions about what discipline methods to use. What guidance can you offer?

Dr. Wolf: One of the things about *adolescence* is that it actually exists. There are a lot of major developmental changes that come together in a very narrow period of time. They get completely new bodies, they develop sexuality, and they get smarter in that they start understanding things through adult eyes. And as part of normal psychological development, it comes into their heads that it is no longer acceptable to them to experience themselves as dependent little kids. In other words, they have to see themselves as independent adult-like beings.

But there's an issue tied to this development change that causes problems for them and their parents. The problem is the parents themselves. You see, teens love their parents and have a strong attachment to them. But being with their parents makes them feel like a dependent little kid and that's a problem. Just being in the same room with their parent, with all the love and attachment still there, it's sort of like a putdown. As I said, being with their parent makes them feel like a little kid and can result in great discomfort.

The teenager might say, "If my parent would just leave, it would cure the problem." And parents are feeling this rejection by their kids and aren't sure why it's happening. They feel as if there are rays emanating from the teenager, pushing them away. Because the vast majority of adolescents did experience attachment to the parents, and were loved by them, it is normal healthy development for these teens to develop a temporary allergy to their parents.

Bill: That is a great illustration of the problem Dr. Wolf. I have an example that I'd like to offer. My daughter was about 13 and she was invited to a roller rink birthday party with a bunch of friends. When I drove to the place top pick her up, I made the mistake of showing up 10 minutes early. When I walked into the roller rink I had this 'loving dad' image in my mind that I would walk up to her and when she saw me, she might say something like, "Hi Dad, it's great to see you." But that dream was short lived. As I approached her, she saw me and quickly covered her eyes as if to block me out of her view. She said, "Oh my gosh Dad, what are you doing here?! This is so embarrassing;

please go wait in the car, I have 10 more minutes to skate."

You've shed some light on this problem, a problem that parents are experiencing raising teenagers and I love how you've characterized it as an allergy. But why does this seem like a new problem for today's parents? Did our parents experience this same problem with us when we were teens or were we different?

Dr. Wolf: I think that we were the same kind of teenagers and I think that most of us did have allergies to our parents. And when adults hear their kids talk back and then think back to their childhood, you hear them say, "I never would have talked to my parents that way," and, "Teens today don't have the same kind of respect for their parents that we did for ours." But what parents don't understand is that what was once considered normal discipline when we were children would now be considered child abuse.

Society has decided that this harsh type of punishment is no longer acceptable and people in general certainly support that. Harsh punishment also gave parents the power to use fear to control their children's behavior. So what do you think happens if you have a teenage child who isn't afraid of her parents? This is the price we pay for this change in acceptable discipline and maybe it's not such a terrible price. The fact is that kids today absolutely talk back more and aren't as immediately obedient as kids were in the past. That means parents must be ready to respond differently to a common, modern-day behavior that was not so common back them.

Bill: It sounds to me that if parents understood this basic concept and relaxed, and didn't take their teen's attitude personally, then the parent/teen relationship could actually improve. That's just the way these things are. So let me ask you Dr. Wolf, in my story with my showing up at my daughter's roller rink party early, if it was a neighbor showing up to pick her up instead, would she have behaved differently?

Dr. Wolf: Yes she would have and she wouldn't have minded that person showing up early at all. You are her parent and you're the one who makes her feel like a little baby. How do you make her feel like a little baby? By just being there, by breathing, and by being alive. It's all because she feels this attachment she has with you. She's had a life of being a little kid with you and now she's allergic to you. When my son was in high school, on some occasions, I would sometimes drive him to the bus stop and he always had me leave him around the bend. He didn't want the humiliation of having the other kids see that he had a parent.

Bill: Another question Dr. Wolf; is there a difference between how boys and girls act out that allergy?

Dr. Wolf: Great question. There is a striking difference. Let's take boys for example, even chatty and friendly boys. They turn 14, they go to their room, close the door, turn on the stereo or computer, and come out for supper and high school graduation. Which is to say that teenage boys deal with the problem of parents making them feel like little babies by creating physical distance and separation. Teenage girls handle it differently. For years they've been bringing their parents, especially their mothers, *I love you mommy* notes with pictures of smiley faces and hearts. The way they deal with their parent allergy is not so much the distance like boys. Instead, they declare their independence moment by moment, in your face!

That can be a big shock to parents. As you related in your story with your daughter, you were imagining the response you had gotten so many years earlier with an "I love you Daddy." But you were shocked with the response of her being embarrassed by your early arrival. This child who once adored me and whose face would light up at my presence now says things like, "Must you?" And you say, "Must you what?" She then says, "Must you talk to me?"

The most important thing for parents to know is that it's not personal and it's temporary. They will outgrow it by the end of adolescence, if not before. It's like a miracle, one day they snap out of it and suddenly turn nice and are fun to be with again. That niceness becomes permanent, even as they move into young adulthood.

Bill: It's funny that you put it that way because that's exactly what my wife and I are experiencing now with our 13-year-old. I sometimes approach her to say something simply conversational and she instantly gives me this disgusting look like I had just done something awful to her by just speaking, you're exactly right.

I hope that this conversation helps some parents cope. This foundational information is the first step in developing a relationship with a teenager and valuable insight into the wiring of our teens that may help us live with these sometimes challenging beings.

SUMMARY:

- It is not unusual for an older child's demeanor to change in the tween or teen years.
- Avoid expecting the same behaviors in your teenager as you saw when they were young.
- During adolescence, teenagers are undergoing many physical and emotional changes.
- Teens must reject the thoughts and feelings that they were once a child.
- Because they feel emotionally attached to the parent, they also appear to reject the parent.
- Some teenagers feel uncomfortable being close, emotionally and physically, to the parent.
- Don't take your teenager's allergy to you personally. It's not you, it's them.
- This is a new problem because it is no longer acceptable to use harsh punishment on children and this kind of treatment used fear to demand compliance from a child.

- Removing fear-based discipline tactics gave rise to teen attitudes and backtalk.
- Parents will get along better with their teens if they relax and try not to be so easily offended.
- Teenagers become allergic only to parents or the primary caregivers, not to other adults.
- This allergy causes teens to feel embarrassed in front of their peers for having parents.
- Boys tend to separate themselves from parents by creating physical distance.
- Girls tend to separate themselves from parents by declaring their independence verbally through arguments.
- Your teen's allergic reaction to you as his or her parent is temporary and will end.
- Don't argue with your teens, give them space and remain calm. See them as going through a - temporary

phase that will end–eventually. They are not being disrespectful, they are declaring their independence.

About the Expert

Anthony E. Wolf, Ph.D.

Dr. Wolf received his Ph.D. in Clinical Psychology from the City University of New York and completed his undergraduate work at Columbia College. For the past twenty-five years he has been in private practice seeing children and adolescents in the Springfield, Massachusetts area. Married, Dr. Wolf is the father of two grown children.

Anthony Wolf is the author of five books on parenting, including *Get Out Of My Life: But first can you drive me and Cheryl to the mall, plus* numerous articles which have appeared in magazines such as: Parents and Family Circle. He has also written a monthly column for Child Magazine. Dr. Wolf is frequently quoted in the national media on issues of parenting. He currently writes a column for the Toronto Globe and Mail. You can learn more about him at www.anthonywolf.com.

Bill Corbett

Interview 2:
Teenagers and the Dangers of Driving

Bill: According to the Centers for Disease Control (CDC), motor vehicle crashes are the leading cause of death for US teenagers. Their statistics show that approximately seven teenagers between 16 and 19 years old die every day from motor vehicle injuries. A father of one of those teens has become a spokesperson for Safety Teen Driving since losing his 17 year old son in a car crash in 2006. Tim Hollister served on the Connecticut state task force that overhauled the state teen driver laws, and has appeared on programs such as: *Raising America* (seen on Headline News).

He is the author of the book *Not So Fast: Parenting Your Teen Through the Dangers of Driving* that Publishers Weekly calls a concise, practical, and potentially lifesaving book that should be required reading for every parent before their teen gets behind the wheel. Mr. Hollister lost his son Reid in a driving accident in 2006, and started a national blog, *From Reid's Dad*, that now attracts more than 20,000 visitors per month.

You've got quite a story to tell and it's one that many parents fear. Most parents can attest to having worked hard to get their children into their teen years, and when they get there, parents feel a bit of relief. We feel like saying "we made it!" but in actuality, not quite. There are still a few more hurdles for us to get over. Tell us your story Tim.

Tim: My son Reid died in a one-car crash on an interstate highway in 2006. About 7 or 8 months later, Connecticut had back-to-back multiple fatality teen driver crashes and at that point, our governor said enough is enough. She appointed a task force to overhaul our teen driver laws which at that point, where among the most lenient in the country, and she appointed me to the task force as a parent. Serving on that task force I received a re-education in the dangers of teen driving. I learned that I really had not been very well informed during the 11 months that I supervised Reid's driving.

But beyond that, I came to the conclusion after studying and working on the task force that most of the literature that's available to parents of teen drivers doesn't explain why teen driving is so dangerous. And more importantly, it doesn't tell parents what they can do, day-by-day, before their teens get behind the wheel to prevent the very predictable—but most dangerous situations. So that became my focus, the literature that was available to parents. As you mentioned, in 2009 I started my national blog for parents called *From Reid's Dad* and it developed a following. Then, about 2 years ago, someone from the National Traffic Safety Organization came to me and said, "You've got enough material on your blog for a book". That blog became a book titled "*Not*

So Fast" which came out about 7 months ago.

Bill: You shared with me a video clip that was on your website. I'd like to share that with our viewers now if it's ok.

Tim: Sure.

Bill: Let's role the film.

(A transcript from the film follows. Watch the film on YouTube by going to https://www.youtube.com/watch?v=5KLii3Mhkps)

Tim: Reid was a bundle of energy. When he got older, he had more friends than we could ever keep track of. He was a people-person right from the get go.

Reid's Sister: He was just so friendly and he genuinely wanted to be friends with everybody. I don't know how else to explain it. He was just the nicest person.

Tim: We remember the day we allowed him to buy a used car. I did what I saw every other parent doing and what I thought I was supposed to do. I took him out on back roads and parking lots on Sunday morning and we did all the skills. I made sure that he understood how a car works. I'd thought I'd touched all the bases. I guess my underlying assumption was that if *I* followed all those rules then ***he'd*** be safe.

I was in Washington, DC when my wife called me and told me that she had heard that Reid and two passengers from our neighborhood had been in a crash. A few minutes later, my wife called me back and she was now in the company of a doctor who lived in our neighborhood. I asked her, "is this serious, do I need to come home?" And she said "you need to come home now."

Reid's sister: I was home that evening when my mom came home and she said "Reid's been in an accident. I'm going to the hospital. Your cousin Emily is coming to stay with you." So you know... when somebody says somebody's been in an accident, I was 14, you always think they're going to get better. They're going to be fine... you know... the doctors are going to fix them.

Tim: So I drove 5 1/2 hours from downtown Washington DC to the hospital and found out that Reid had died two hours earlier. We spent a lot of time looking for a car that was safe, and he didn't crash the entire 11 months that he was driving before his fatal crash, so I think that was my mind set; no news was good news.

Reid's Sister: I went there and I sat with my mom and we cried. I realized that there is a hole that is never going to be filled. I think the hardest thing was when we were figuring out what clothes he was going to be buried in. So I picked out his khaki shorts and his bright pink polo, his favorite thing to wear. You know... what does a 17-year-old want to be buried in?

Tim: The experts say it takes three to five years to become a relatively safe driver, so compare that to the 40 hours that we require. That's a drop in the bucket in terms of getting a license. When teens have a reason to get to a certain destination, they're probably going to get there safely. It's the joy riding where we see the crashes with passengers. Don't think that your obligation to your teen is just helping them get their license; that's really when we need to begin. If you've got a teen whose been driving for a year but they're not ready, just because the law says they can have passengers doesn't mean it's a good idea. The laws are the minimum; parents need to figure out what it is that needs to be done above and beyond the law.

(End of film clip excerpt)

Bill: It's not easy sharing your story and I'm so glad that you did. So many teen lives may be saved because of Reid and because of your willingness to talk about it. Awareness in anything is what keeps us safer. It allows people to make changes and if we don't have that awareness, we sometimes get stuck in our unconscious world. I really appreciate you being willing to do that and to tell Reid's story. So I have a couple of questions if you don't mind. Why is driving so dangerous for teens?

Tim: The main reason, and this is relatively new science that has come out of the last 10 years, is that the human brain is not fully developed until we reach about age 22-25 and the last function that develops in the brain is judgment and restraint. Which is why teens are drawn to danger, but they don't really understand the risks. If you apply that to driving, the first question is, "why do we allow teens to drive at 16?" Well, because they've been doing that for 50 - 60 years and this science is relatively new.

If the driving age where now based on this new science, it would be at least 21 maybe 22. Parents need to understand, this is a characteristic of teens that they just can't change. It's a danger they have to factor into their management of parenting teens on a daily basis. Your son or daughter can be a boy scout or a girl scout or a straight A student, it doesn't matter. He or she doesn't have 10,000 hours behind the wheel yet. It's just something you have to deal with; it's part of the danger.

Another reason that's very important is that new drivers look at the perimeter of the car. Their trying hard not to hit anything and don't know enough to look down the road into developing traffic situations, which is how you avoid a crash. And then third, we train our teens on local roads and familiar streets in compact cars, but then they drive an SUV or a high performance vehicle on the freeway into major cities. They are learning to navigate and drive at the same time. It's a very formidable challenge and parents need to understand just how dangerous it is.

Bill: And you're right. With my education in clinical psychology, I try to help parents understand that the prefrontal cortex (the very front of the brain), as you said, is not completely developed. This is where their judgment comes from, the area that helps them judge their actions - such as the dangers associated with behaviors and actions that hurt them, whether it's driving or sexting or anything. What happens, what I think researchers have shown through brain scans, is that the part of the brain that draws them toward taking risks, lights up brighter and over powers the under developed parts of the brain. The teens don't understand that their parent draws boundaries or limits to help keep them safe. Instead, the teen gets mad at the parent and says something like, "What's the matter? You don't trust me?"

Tim: This is not science that you and I learned in high school or college. It's relatively new because of the brain scans.

Bill: Tell us about the graduated driver laws.

Tim: Graduated driver laws exist in most states now in varying degrees, but basically the graduated driver law is letting out the tether for a teen driver in small increments, targeting the most dangerous situations. The most prominent one is no passengers for the first 6 months or year of driving. Then there are curfews, night driving limitations, requirements of seat belts, no electronic devices, and no texting, nothing of that kind. It's all aimed at making sure that the danger or the exposure to danger is minimized until the teen really has a significant amount of experience under their belt—at least a year.

Bill: It's very important they get small increments of driving opportunities that allow the brain to begin developing. You also said something about purposeful driving as oppose to joy riding, which was brought out on the video clip. Tell us a little more.

Tim: When I bring this up to parents, they kind of have an 'aha' moment. It's just below our consciousness. If teens have a reason and a timetable to get to a particular place - going to school, going to sports practice, going to a job, they're going to drive conservatively and safely and they'll probably get there on time and without any problem. It's the joy riding with multiple teens in a car for fun. That's where we see the peer pressure and distraction, the misconduct and the reckless driving. In central Connecticut as an example, in the summer of 2013 we had 10 teen driver fatal crashes and 8 out of the 10 involved joy riding - multiple teens in a car out for fun. So that's where the problem is.

Bill: And this is education that we definitely need to get parents to understand. Being a parent of a teenager is hard enough, but when our kids start driving, that's when our hair really starts turning grey.

SUMMARY:
- Teens and young adults under 22 years of age have poor judgment and restraint.
- Teaching your teen to drive isn't enough; more education and awareness is required.
- Just because a teen has a license doesn't mean they're completely trained to drive.

- Teen drivers haven't developed the ability to look 'down the road' yet for pending dangers.
- Avoid allowing teens to joyride; purposeful driving with a destination only.

About the Expert

Tim Hollister

Mr. Hollister has become a national authority and spokesperson for safer teen driving since losing his 17 year old son Reid in a car crash in 2006. After serving on a Connecticut task force in 2007 that overhauled the state's teen driver laws, in 2009 Tim launched *From Reid's Dad*, a national blog for parents of teen drivers that now attracts more than 20,000 visitors per month and is relied upon by traffic safety organizations, driving schools, and parents throughout the country. Tim has appeared on national and regional programs such as "Raising America" on HLN and "Mr. Dad."

In 2013, Tim's book *Not So Fast: Parenting Your Teen Through the Dangers of Driving* was released by the Chicago Review Press. Publishers Weekly has called the book "A concise, practical and potentially life-saving book that should be required reading for every parent before their teen gets behind the wheel." Tim was named the AAA Club of Southern New England's Traffic Safety Hero of the Year in 2013, and in 2010 he received the U.S. Department of Transportation's National Public Service Award, the nation's highest civilian honor for traffic safety. Tim is an environmental attorney and lives in Bloomfield, CT.

Interview 3:
Teens and Marijuana

Bill: According to the 2009 national survey on drug use and health, on average, nearly 7,000 young people from ages 12-17 try marijuana for the first time every single day. Interestingly enough, the rate of their peers disapproving of them using it increased from 84.7% in 2002 to 87% in 2009. This statistic shows that peer pressure to avoid the drug is on the increase, but what can parents do if they discover their teen is using marijuana? Here is my interview with parent coach and therapist Susan Epstein who has some valuable experience in this area.

It's an incredible challenge being a parent today. We have to stay up to date on the things that influence our teenagers; we have to know where our teenagers go and also, who they hang out with. A huge factor is the influence exerted on our teens by their peers, especially peers who have parents who use very few, or have no boundaries or limits in their homes. And of course, the pressure to experiment with marijuana is one thing that our teens are likely to be exposed to by their friends.

Susan: Yes, it's everywhere and it doesn't matter where you live, what your neighborhood looks like, or how much money you make. Kids are going to feel pressure from other kids and parents need to be super vigilant about staying connected to their kids to offset that influence. I've worked with a lot of families and many kids will experiment; it's going to happen. They'll go through the phase of trying a drug, but it won't stick with them, and they won't become consumed with it.

Then there are other children who will use it and continue to use it. A lot of times, kids diagnosed with ADHD will use it and say it makes them feel better or it helps them concentrate. Unfortunately for others, they will begin using it and it will consume them. Their grades will start to go down and it will affect their relationship with the rest of the family. Because of the shameful secret they're carrying around, they begin to disconnect with their parents.

Bill: What are some possible signs a parent can watch for to know if their child is smoking marijuana?

Susan: Number one is to watch your child's grades for sudden negative changes, and number two is if your child suddenly goes immediately to his room whenever he arrives home; he doesn't want you to see his face because he's high. You may need to do some investigation if your kid comes in the front door, runs up to his bedroom, slams the door, and then avoids contact with you. And even though I used HE in my example, it can be girls or boys.

A classic scenario is the parent going to the teenager's bedroom door and speaking to him through the door, "Is everything OK?

Where were you?" The child then responds with something like, "I'm fine Mom; I was just with friends, why do you need to know?" Mom then says, "I need to know where you are and it's my job to know." The teenager quickly gets defensive and they argue. It's obvious to the parent that the teenager is hiding something.

Bill: That becomes a real challenge since teenagers have a secretive nature anyway. It's now intensified because they have something even more to hide from the parents.

Susan: It is; it's really hard. It's even harder for kids who don't feel understood by their parents and then parents are feeling like they don't really know who this person is who's living in their house. They're now saying something like, "I thought this was my sweet and kind little child, but now they've turned into this person that I don't even know anymore."

Bill: Let's talk about what parents can do if they suspect that their child may be experimenting with marijuana.

Susan: The first thing to do is not to overreact. Too many parents pull out the classic punishment of grounding their teen. Some may even threaten to call the police; it's all overreaction. I suggest that parents take a different approach and maybe even use a little humor. If you do, you're more likely to get past the normal rebellion that teens demonstrate toward parents.

Let's say you found it in the bedroom dresser drawer. A typical hiding place is beneath the underwear. You're the mom who is still doing your teen's laundry and you're putting the clothes away and you find it. I would just put it on the kitchen table and leave it there. Then your teen comes home from school and they are shocked to see it sitting there. Don't say anything, just leave it there. Let it sit with them for a while.

It's way more powerful when you allow the guilt inside of them to speak to them, rather than you starting the conversation. They will be thinking to themselves, "Oh my gosh, I broke a huge rule. Now my parents know!" They must own it and deal with it. Avoid being the parent that races in and scolds and lectures. There is magic around giving this incident some space and time. Then when you've calmed down and your teen has been hiding for a while, announce to your kid that it's time to talk.

Some people might think that my next suggestion is a little out there, but I say, "Do it anyway". Tell your teen that they must write an essay titled *The Teenage Brain and Marijuana*. It must be a minimum of 250 words double-spaced and it must be a B paper. As a result, they cannot go anywhere except to school and back until that paper is turned in. Deliver these instructions without getting angry and certainly no yelling.

They'll probably procrastinate for two or three days and probably mope around the house and maybe even act like they're mad at you. If they give you any grief, just say to them, "Give me the paper and then we can talk about this and move on." When they finally give you the paper, you can sit down and have a calm discussion. Be sure and ask them, "Tell me what you learned?" It will be a great beginning to a solid discussion.

Another thing you can do if you feel you need to, is to drug test them. You can buy these tests in most drug stores or you can buy them online at TestMyTeen.com. There is even a swab test so that you don't have to do a urine test. The urine test is a bit intrusive and uncomfortable for some moms with teenage boys. If your teen pulls the "I know my civil rights, you can't touch me" line, all you have to tell him is that his refusal is an instant admission of guilt.

Once you swab test your teen, you're going to test him again in 30 days because the THC from the drug stays in the body for 28 days. You're going to say, "I'm going to test you on day 31, 32 or 33, to see if you're clean and by the way, I'm holding the keys to the car until then." Some kids might even declare, "You can't control me and stop me from smoking weed." You can then tell him that he might be able to smoke without you knowing it, but as long as you know he's not driving, you won't have to worry about him getting into an accident. We certainly don't want our kids doing drugs, but it's really their safety and well-being we care about most.

Bill: Wow, really creative ideas for parents. I want to go back and revisit something you said earlier that I think was one of the most important tips. You advised parents to RELAX. I don't want to glaze over that because it's so important. The more relaxed parents remain when dealing with this issue, the more success they are going to have with the whole problem.

Susan: Absolutely.

Bill: Unfortunately, what happens too often is that the parents freak out and immediately get angry, yell, and punish the teen. Your advice of holding the keys until they test clean is a very fair consequence and not a punishment. Handling this problem by being fair and respectful will increase your success with getting what you want—your teen to understand the problem and to hopefully stop.

Susan: Yes, I like to call it *mindful robotic parenting*. Be a robot. Don't let them see how upset you are and if you have to, use humor to deflect some of what's going on.

Bill: Some excellent advice here Susan, thank you. For parents of school aged children and teens, I hope that you've picked up some great tips that will empower you to take action if it becomes necessary.

SUMMARY:
- Use peer pressure to your advantage by influencing your teen to hang out with kids who do not use marijuana.
- Get to know the parents of teenagers that your teen hangs out with.
- If your teens have friends who have little or no boundaries and limits at home, establish a rule to always have those friends hang out at your home.
- Drugs are a cure for boredom.

Therefore, be sure your teens are occupied with out-of-school activities they enjoy to keep them interested.

- A sudden drop in your teenager's grades is a reason to take notice and investigate what might be causing the change.
- If you notice a change in your teenager's behavior of going directly to his or her room upon arriving home, there is a possibility that they could be hiding something from you.
- As the parent, you have the right to know where your teenager goes and where they've been.
- While teens do strive to increase their privacy from parents, the amount of that privacy should be within reason.
- When approaching your teen about something you have a concern about, remain calm and avoid overreacting.
- Although it may be easier said than done, using light humor when addressing concerns with your teen can be effective.
- If you should find marijuana in your

teen's room, clothing, or possessions, put it somewhere out in the open so there is no doubt about it having been found. If you have more than one child and/or younger children, this may not be an acceptable option for you. It might be a good opportunity however, to have a discussion with your younger children about drugs.

- Instead of expressing your anger about finding the drug, have your teen write an essay to get them thinking about the consequences of using drugs. Make sure you provide them with a clear set of instructions on the topic, word count, and quality of the essay they need to write.

- Always avoid scolding, lecturing, yelling, and punishing a teenager. Consequences, when implemented correctly, are far more effective at changing behavior. Punishment demands obedience; consequences permit choice.

- Create space and time before addressing concerns with a teenager;

it will give you time to calm down and them a chance to think things over.

- Affordable drug testing kits are available from most drugstore or www.TestMyTeen.com

---

About the Expert

Susan Epstein

Susan graduated from Clark University in Worcester, MA in 1980, where she earned a B.A. degree in Sociology and Spanish with a minor in Psychology. She pursued her M.S.W. from the University of California at Berkeley School of Social Welfare. She completed training in 2003 with the internationally accredited Coaches Training

Institute. Being bilingual with English and Spanish has enabled Susan to work with multiple cultures throughout her career.

Susan travels nationally, presenting seminars on Challenging and Resistant Children and Adolescents for PESI. Susan has appeared frequently on television, radio, in all the national parenting magazines and websites. She is also a published author of 7 parenting books, including *55 Creative Approaches for Challenging & Resistant Children and Adolescents*. Susan offers a certified parent coach training program with Christian Mickelsen, teaching the skill set of Parent Coaching as well as the marketing skills to launch the business. Sign up to receive her FREE Special Report on how to put a stop to your child's bad behavior immediately. You can visit Susan's website at: www.ParentingPowers.com.

Bill Corbett

Interview 4:
Violence and the Male Teenager

Bill: According to an article in Psychology Today, parents should know where their teen boys are at all times and they should not succumb to the "You don't trust me" smoke screen. Research has shown that the lack of supervision and youth violence are two leading factors that contribute to deaths among young people.

Jim Bouchard transformed himself from a dropout, drug-abuser, and failure, to a successful entrepreneur and black belt in martial arts. He travels nationally, presenting his philosophy of the black belt mind set for both parent and corporate audiences. He's the author of the Amazon best seller, *Think Like a Black Belt*, a book that takes you inside the mind of the black belt to develop the confidence, courage, discipline, focus, and leadership you need for excellence in your personal and professional life.

Jim, talk to us about teen violence. I'm guessing that influence might come from TV and video games, but what do you think is the fundamental cause of it?

Jim: It's really very simple. If we were doing a better job of instilling values in our youngest people across the board, we wouldn't have this issue. The solution to the problem is very, very simple, and we've completely over complicated it. This is why I'm on the soap box about discipline along with responsibility and respect. If we got back to addressing all three of those values we'd solve most of the problems that we're facing right now.

Now for the argument; we've got kids that are born to single parent families and many of those kids have little or no parental supervision. Then, the schools are not able to impose the values as we would. But those are just excuses and we've been making those excuses for a longtime. We've got more conferences, we've got more meetings, we've got more studies, and the root of the problem is exactly the same. We know who the bully is and we know who the violent offenders are. I've been doing some work with youth in prisons and the stories that these kids tell would amaze you.

Bill: I was talking to a teacher over the weekend and he said he polled his class to see how many of the boys play grand theft auto. He was stunned when more than half of the teen boys raised their hands. Personally, I wish there was a way to make parents more accountable. And while you and I may not let our kids play those games, they are influenced by those who do.

Jim: Parents are still the greatest influence in a child's life, that's the way it is. Of course peer pressure is certainly there. We've talked about the issue of violent video games but I don't believe that is necessarily the cause of a lot of these problems. It certainly is a stimulant though. But censorship isn't the answer either. We must fall back on holding people accountable, and not just the parents. We've got to hold the kids accountable because they will be at some point. I'd rather hold them accountable in the 6th grade than hold them accountable at the Youth Detention Center.

Bill: You're absolutely right. Sometimes when I'm working in my office, I'll turn on my scanner to listen in to what's happening around town. I'm amazed with the number of calls our local police department gets because a child is being violent to their mother, she can't get him to go to school, or she can't get him to get out of his room. We're using taxpayers' money and tying up our law enforcement when we need them available for real emergencies.

Jim: I'm the biggest advocate of individual freedom that you're ever going to find, but if you want to have that freedom, you have to have accountability. I'm working on a new book with the working title *Knock it Off.*

That's what I say to parents. If you can't produce children that you can take care adequately, then knock it off; stop having babies. I know that's not a popular stance to make. But really, the answer is that simple. We've got to get back to the simplicity of the problem.

Bill: No one seems to want to talk about parental responsibility today. For example, how many times have we seen the talk show featuring a mom and her teenage daughter, both crying and demanding justice for a predator because the daughter was sexually harassed, raped, or abused? Then we find out that she connected with this guy on social media from her computer in her bedroom, something she was able to do because there was no supervision. What if there were laws that would penalize parents for their contribution to the problem?

Jim: I encourage parents to spy on their kids, not that they need permission to do it of course. I'm a staunch advocate of it. There are so many software options today for hand-held devices and computers. There are no reasons NOT to do it. I met a woman whose daughter was abducted. She has now come out as an advocate for one of these programs. I would much rather see parents staying on top of what their children are doing, rather than being an absent parent.

Through forums like your television show, I will stand up and make myself heard on these and other less popular stances. My new book *Knock It Off* is going to tackle these and other bigger social issues that I think have some clear solutions if we have the courage to face them. There are some simple solutions that are sometimes the most difficult to implement. And on the other side of the spectrum, there are these broad reaching solutions that do nothing but create unintended consequences, and they end up punishing more people than they benefit. Although it's not popular, in my new book I talk about getting back to grabbing some folks by the scuff of the neck and saying to them, "Look, if you want be a parent, you're accountable to that. You must do your job right!"

Bill: In opposition to having parents control or monitor their children's activities online, there is a growing movement to put the Internet in the hands of children starting in infancy. These same folks urge parents not to monitor their children and to give them privacy and freedom. What are your thoughts on this?

Jim: It's actually going to make me sick! I know you're a great advocate of encouraging parents to create a better balance with media, technology, and the Internet. I like to tell parents that the greatest thing we can give to our children is our attention. The greatest gift you can give your child is your time and your full attention, and it doesn't necessarily mean that you have to be there all the time physically. I know some very successful parents of military families and folks in the music business. When they are home, they're fully present when they are there and that's the key.

Bill: It's amazing and heartbreaking when we see families all plugged into technology and not conversing or giving each other their full attention.

Jim: Don't get me started on that one. That unfortunately, is the wall we put up and that's related to the problem with the violence issue as well. I do a program for kids and parents called, *Don't Stand by, Stand Up*. It's become too frequent to see videos posted online in which a kid is getting beaten up. There is one that went viral recently in which all the kids standing around are videotaping it and no one is calling 911. That to me is a sickness, that's where we have to get into the homes and schools and hold someone accountable.

Bill: Do you have some guidelines for parents and other adults? We certainly want them to step up and take responsibility, but do you have any suggestions for parents?

Jim: Yes. Teach children to be disciplined

in whatever they do. My personal problem with drugs came about because I didn't have any meaningful and purposeful habits in place; that's how I define discipline. It's up to parents to train their children to become disciplined through boundaries and routines. We have to put an end to this attitude that some parents have of not wanting to be too pushy with their kids and allowing them to do whatever they want, whenever they want to do it.

Parents also need to step up and demonstrate the *Pay it Forward* movement of doing acts of kindness to others. Doing so removes the time and space of negative things that kids see and think about. Don't be afraid to upset your child if you introduce new things in the family routine to get them thinking in a positive direction.

SUMMARY:
- The magazine Psychology Today suggests that parents should always know where their teen boys are.
- Parents shouldn't succumb to the

"You Don't Trust Me!" smoke screen teens use to get parents to ease up on their supervision.

- Parents must do a better job of instilling values in their teens.
- Don't let your children and teens play video games such as Grand Theft Auto.
- Single parenting is tough, but it's not an acceptable excuse for easing up on supervision of kids and teens.
- Playing violent video games may not be the key reason for violence among youth, but a lack of influence from the parents might be.
- Teenagers who incite violence must be held accountable for their actions.
- Monitoring your child's activity on the Internet is not popular, but the reasons for doing it outweigh the reasons not to do it.
- The greatest gifts we can give our children are our time and undivided attention.
- Train your child to be disciplined in

whatever activities they do, through boundaries and routines.

- Demonstrate the act of *Paying it Forward* as a model of kindness for your child to learn from.
- Fill your children's thinking with positive acts and routines.

About the Expert

Jim Bouchard

Jim Bouchard increases engagement and productivity, and develops leadership at all levels of your organization by teaching your people how to THINK Like a BLACK BELT. As a speaker, corporate trainer and author of the Amazon bestseller *THINK Like a BLACK BELT*, Jim tours nationally presenting his philosophy of Black Belt Mindset for corporate and conference audiences. He's a regular guest on TV and radio programs across the country and internationally. For more information visit www.ThatBlackBeltGuy.com.

Interview 5:
How to Connect with Your Teenager

Bill: One thing that frustrates today's parents of teenagers is that the teens might get away with behaviors that would not have been tolerated by parents in past generations. But we have to understand that the world has changed and so has the modern day teen. This means that parents of teens must update their parenting skill set to be more effective parents.

This is the second of two interviews I did with Dr. Anthony Wolf, a practicing clinical psychologist who has worked with adolescents for over 30 years and is the author of one of my favorite books on teens, *Get Out Of My Life: But First Could You Drive Me And Cheryl To The Mall*.

Dr. Wolf, what does healthy, daily interaction with a teen look like? What should parents be striving to do to make life easier living with their teenager?

Dr. Wolf: First of all, we need to understand that modern day teenagers aren't afraid of their parents like we were of ours. This is because, over the years, parents stopped using harsh punishment and fear to control their kids. When this happened, kids—especially teenagers, began standing up to their parents more. They were no longer afraid of their parents.

Many are also likely to badger their parents continuously until they get what they want. If the parent says, "I'm sorry sweetheart but I can't drive you over to your friend's house. It's really too late." The teenager is then likely to say, "But you don't understand I have to go over her house. You have to let me." If they don't get their way, they will go on and on until they get the parent to give in and they get what they want.

Making life with a teenager a little easier

means developing the courage to say what you need to say and standing firm with your decision. It also means not getting angry about their persistence. The adult has to be the one to calmly have their say and then end the discussion if necessary, because the teen usually won't.

Bill: So what I'm hearing you say is, number one, remain calm and hear them out. Then state your position or decision clearly. If the teenager persists and doesn't accept your answer, then it's up to the parent to end the interaction because the teen isn't likely to.

Dr. Wolf: Yes. One mistake that parents make is trying hard to get their teen to understand why they made the decision they did. It becomes a waste of time in many cases because the teen doesn't care about the parent's reasons. It then becomes a battle in which each side is attempting to be heard. The teen is trying to change the parent's mind, and the parent is trying to get the teen to understand why he or she made the decision.

It is extremely rare for a teen to suddenly say, "I see your point, thanks for explaining it to me." Instead, they have what I call a teenage tantrum. The best thing for parents to do is to give their teen a chance to be heard, announce their decision, then disengage by walking away.

One big problem with remaining in that space and trying to get the teen to understand is when the teen begins to increase the intensity of their persuasion. When they feel they are losing, they use revenge as a last attempt. The teenager gets nasty and says mean things to the parent such as, "I hate you", or "You're the worst parent in the world", and all sorts of other statements that are hurtful to the parent.

Then the parent says, "Now what am I supposed to do when my teen begins hurling those insults at me?"

The parent then responds with something like, "How dare you talk to me that way." They feel they have to say something in response to those remarks. The teenager comes back with, "I will too talk to you that way, I'll talk to you anyway I want", and the parent says, "Oh no you won't!" Finally, the parent begins to hurt back by making threats or even punishment.

The real skill in parenting a teenager is learning to remain calm and then disengage if the teenager decides to continue the tantrum.

Bill: I've noticed how parents feel so much resentment when their teen throws fits. The teenager gets mad because he or she can't have a Facebook page or can't go to the big party that supposedly every teenager in the world is going to. Then the parent feels resentment because they think about all the things they've done for their child and this adds fuel to the fire. The parent thinks to them self, "I've done so much for you. I have practically gone into debt so you can have all the things you have, and you have the audacity to talk to me this way!"

Dr. Wolf: That's a wonderful example,

which reinforces why it is so important for the parent to learn to disengage and walk away. The best thing a parent can do in response to hearing the hurtful remarks is to say, "If you, my beloved teenage child, are going to act like this towards me, then I take the position that I don't have to listen to this, and have the power to walk away and not hang around with you right now."

And teenagers have the skills to keep ratcheting it up another notch. The parent walks away and now the teen is saying something like, "You're not listening to me. You have to listen to me!" and sometimes follow the parent. If the parent attempts to remain in that spot and rattle off all the things they've done for the teen, they are going to accomplish nothing. The teen is certainly not going to say, "Thanks for pointing out all the wonderful things you've done for me." Instead, they either won't listen to it, or they may even find fault with the parent, or all the things they've done for them. Then the parent feels even more hurt.

The parent must take charge and disengage and walk away. If they feel they have to say something, they could say, "I understand that you're mad, but I'm not going to stand here and listen to this abuse." They can't allow themselves to get sucked into the destructive encounter.

Bill: What you just described is hard for a parent. We want a peaceful and loving resolution and want the uncomfortable moment to smooth over. We parents live in somewhat of a dream world at times. What we really want is for the teenager to say, "You're right Mom, I don't really have to go to that party, and you have done so many wonderful things for me" and then have it end with a warm hug. But that's certainly unlikely to happen.

Dr. Wolf, what other suggestions do you have for parents to connect with the modern day teenager? Most parents know how to connect with a younger child, but what can they do with an older child?

Dr. Wolf: Parents don't seem to realize that

their teenagers really like to be with them. I know that it might be hard to understand this because these kids are in the normal mode of rejecting their parents, but they really do like to be with them. Then parents make it even harder by their constant reminders and nagging. Parents say things like, "Did you do your homework? Did you do your chores? Did you put your clothes in the laundry?'

If the parents can just be with their teens and be quiet and just listen, their teens may actually like being with them. I encourage adults to try and suppress the parent voice in their heads and just be a good listener. Learn to remain quiet and if you have to say something, ask questions about their likes, dislikes, school, hobbies, and friends. And be satisfied with their answers, no matter how vague. Avoid asking 'why' so much and avoid criticizing.

Bill: You make some very good points. The strategy in connecting with teens is to just be with them. Occasionally, I would ask permission to enter my teen daughter's room by knocking on the door and asking, "Mind if I like, hang out with you for few minutes?" One day she was painting her toenails on her bed and she was listening to some of her music. I knocked and asked if I could come in. She said "I guess" with a little bit of annoyance and I sat there for a few minutes. I then asked her if she would paint my toenails. We had one of the best moments together, that I'll remember forever.

You're right Dr. Wolf, developing new skills to connect with our teens means shutting off the parental voice in our heads and learning to be with them more in silence and also being genuinely curious. Even though we mean well, they don't want to hear our reminders and nagging.

Dr. Wolf: Parents need to learn how to get along with their teens, rather than the other way around. They also have to have a sense of humor. Some parents do take themselves too seriously.

Bill: Thank you Dr. Wolf. This gives parents a place to start in reconnecting with their teens. Make the effort to reconnect, but learn to walk away even when that seems like the most unlikely thing to do.

SUMMARY

- Our teenagers behave differently today than we did as teenagers.
- Removing fear and harsh punishment from discipline removes a teen's fear of the parent.
- Some of the discipline our parents used cannot be used today.
- It is normal for some teenagers to badger their parents to try and wear them down so they can get what they want.
- Parents should not get angry at their teenager's persistence to get what they want.
- Develop the skill of remaining calm when listening to your teenager's requests or demands.
- It's OK to explain your reason for your decision, but don't expect your

teenager to agree or understand.

- Avoid responding to hurtful comments from your teenager; don't take them personal.
- Develop the skill of walking away when you've heard enough.
- Avoid arguing with your teenager. Simply hear them out and then disengage by physically removing yourself.
- As hard as it may be, let your teenager have the last word.
- Resist feeling resentful because your teen wants more and appears ungrateful for what you've done.
- Allow teenage 'tantrums' to occur without trying to control or extinguish them.
- Your teenager really wants to be with you, but doesn't want to hear your nagging and reminding.
- Learn to turn off the 'parental voice' in your head and just be with your teenager.
- Sharpen your skills for remaining

quiet and listening.

- Be curious about your teenager's likes, dislikes, and interests.

About the Expert

Anthony E. Wolf, Ph.D.

Dr. Wolf received his Ph.D. in Clinical Psychology from the City University of New York and completed his undergraduate work at Columbia College. For the past twenty-five years he has been in private practice seeing children and adolescents in the Springfield, Massachusetts area. Married, Dr. Wolf is the father of two grown children.

Anthony Wolf is the author of five books on parenting, including *Get Out Of My Life: But first can you drive me and Cheryl to the mall, plus* numerous articles which have appeared in magazines such as: Parents and Family Circle. He has also written a monthly column for Child Magazine. Dr. Wolf is frequently quoted in the national media on issues of parenting. He currently writes a column for the Toronto Globe and Mail. You can learn more about him at www.anthonywolf.com.

Bill Corbett

Interview 6:
Dangers Awaiting Teens on the Internet

Bill: According   to   the   website www.childrenonline.org, a comprehensive consulting company that provides up to date information about the use and impact of technology   on   child   and   adolescent development, nearly 83% of all students record having Internet access from their bedrooms, but only 16% record having some sort of web filtering, parental control software on their computer.

This means that most children have Internet access behind the closed doors of their bedroom without any parental supervision or oversight. About one out of every four students reports having made a friend online whom they've never met in person, yet the contact from a stranger was selected as the event that made students feel the most uncomfortable.

I interviewed two experts who have some cautions for parents. David Ryan Polgar is a writer, attorney, and college professor at Tunxis Community College. He has been featured on MSN and Fox News, and recently delivered a Tedx talk on mental obesity. David is also the author of the book *Wisdom in the Age of Twitter: A Fun and Quick Guide to Better Thinking.*

Dr. David Greenfield is the founder of the Center for Internet and Technology Addiction. He is considered one of the world's leading authorities on Internet and computer behavior in digital media technology. Dr. Greenfield's recent work is focused on why digital technologies are so addictive and on how we, as a society, can use technology in a more balanced and healthy manner.

The shadow side of the Internet is something that I think presents huge risks to our kids, but because the chances of something bad happening to a child is low, I think that parents make keeping their children safe while online a low priority. I think they treat Internet safety as no big deal. But I ask parents "Why should we be dismissing that risk to our kids? Isn't even a small chance that something bad could happen to them online enough of a reason to take proactive action?" So tell us what you mean by the phrase you used, "*the shadow side of the Internet.*"

Dr. Greenfield: The shadow side is the dark side. I'll be going in two different directions with this. The first one is what I refer to as the *deep Internet*, a section that requires specialized browsers and systems to get access to it. In that area of the Internet, there's stuff that is so illegal and dangerous that I don't even want to talk about it on the show. That's one danger that children face and they could stumble on it.

But even without going to the deep Internet, they're able to access the world's most potent and powerful pornographic and violent content with just a click of a mouse. One of the things that we find with addiction is that the shorter the latency between the time that you ingest the substance and the time that you receive the intoxication, the more addictive that behavior becomes. So with faster Internet feeds, better processors, and the fact that they can click and see something that's powerful and potent from a content perspective, an addictive medium like the Internet produces this amplification of danger that we are seeing.

David: It's not just intentionally going 10 degrees to the right to try and find something that may be scandalous. It's just one Google search away from landing on something incredibly inappropriate, especially for children. I think that's something parents need to understand. It's not that hard for a child to enter one search that might seem kind of ambiguous or not scandalous at all, and then just a couple of clicks away, they're into some darker territory.

Dr. Greenfield: I could give examples involving some of our patients where there has been legal involvement, where they did a search and it took them to a site that is government connected or government sponsored. Then they look at it or download information, a video, or photos that are illegal in nature and then they're in trouble. It doesn't matter whether it was an innocent mistake or by accident. What David is saying is that any adult or child is just one click away from potential trouble. You don't know what you are getting yourself into.

Bill: You mentioned a couple of issues… serious issues. I'd like to add something that I consider an additional problem, especially for children. Most devices come with a camera installed. The additional risk is that children are being connected by camera to anybody in the world. If we look at dangerous sites such as Chatroullete and Omegle, kids with unlimited Internet access in their bedrooms don't understand the consequences. They want to connect and they want to have friends. They're suddenly discovering that just by logging on, they can get a new friend using the video camera.

David: I agree. Part of that problem is that pictures now stay out on the Internet indefinitely, and children aren't making wise decisions because of their age, their background, their cognitive ability, and their life experience. Just one misguided photo can really follow a person around. A topic that just came up in the news recently was this onslaught of what they are calling 'revenge sites'.

On these sites, a person posts an inappropriate photo that was intended for just one person or to keep private. Then, an ex-boyfriend or ex-girlfriend posts this photo and also attaches contact information to it. Right now this type of incident is in a legal gray area because people do have certain first amendment rights. But it's very unclear on what anyone can actually do about this. It really comes down to the responsibility of the parent or the child in not uploading these kinds of photographs to begin with.

Bill: What about the problem that's been termed as 'catfishing?'

Dr. Greenfield: The guy behind that TV show developed that based on a true experience. One of the things we learned from the original research that we did was that 50% of people that go online admit to lying about some personal aspect of themselves online. Usually it's what they do for a living, what they look like, their height, and even in some cases, their gender. Fifty percent of that number is probably an underestimate because some people are lying about the lie. So you can see where we're going with this. When people meet online and develop cyber relationships that are only online, you really don't know what you are getting.

Bill: The term 'catfishing' derives from the movie documentary *Catfish* (2011) about a woman who created a false Facebook identity and used it to draw a 24-year-old man into a relationship. His filmmaker brother and a friend follow him on camera as he attempts to track down and meet the woman. But what he finds is not what he was expecting.

David: It's very easy to create a false identity. Two years before the movie *Catfish*, there is a well-known case in which two teenage girls who were best friends, ended up having a falling out. The mother of one of those girls got very involved, created a fake account on MySpace as a teenage boy, and engaged the other girl in a romantic relationship. Then at some point, the mother masquerading as a teenage boy, ended the relationship and suggested that the girl kill herself. The teenage girl took the breakup so hard that she followed the advice and committed suicide.

Dr. Greenfield: There are other horror stories where people have taken on personas pretending to be someone else. A documentary was made about a woman who took on her daughter's identity. Then she met a man online who fell in love with her. Another man got involved, which created a love triangle, and that resulted in a shooting. People actually do get hurt in these situations. And that's not to mention the other psychological and physiological consequences of embedding oneself in social media too much. And because kids are sitting still in front of computer screens for longer periods of time, we're seeing increases in obesity, hypertension, diabetes, repetitive motion injuries, and deep thrombosis, all the side effects of sedentary behavior.

Bill: And of course, this increases the opportunities for bullying. When we were kids, bullying usually ended around 3:15 in the afternoon, the time we arrived home from school. There was a level of safety there. But thanks to the Internet and all it offers, bullying is now taking place 24 hours a day.

David: There's never really a time that we can easily get away from it all and relax. I think we're always going to see the natural tendency for children to want to stay in touch with peers using social media networks; the very same place that they could potentially be bullied.

Dr. Greenfield: That's where our kids are hanging out now, so that becomes the big dilemma and parents are struggling with it. Our kids are hanging out in cyberspace.

Bill: Yes, it's the modern day playground for our kids.

Dr. Greenfield: And because the Internet has become accepted as the modern day child's playground, we can't just say to parents "Please get your kids off the Internet or social media networks." They find that request unreasonable and unfair. It really becomes an issue of balance and monitoring.

Bill: The title of one of my recent blog posts was, *Please Don't Buy Your Kids a Data Plan*. The message in it was that children with smart phones are likely to share inappropriate material they find on the Internet with children who do not have unlimited access to these devices, like my kids didn't have. I've taken a lot of heat from those who take the position that our kids are digital citizens and we need to help them to adapt to the real world and all that it has to offer as early as possible.

Dr. Greenfield: But there is a backlash brewing and David and I have talked about this. We need more education and public awareness now, rather than waiting to see the effects of the overuse and abuse of technology.

SUMMARY:
- Go to the website ChildrenOnline.org for more information on this topic.
- Refrain from allowing your children to have Internet access in their bedroom.
- Computers that your children use should be located in a common area you can monitor.
- Even small risks to your child's safety and well-being should be eliminated.

- One innocent Google search can land kids on dangerous websites.
- Lean how to disable the camera on your child's laptop.
- Two dangerous websites for kids are chatroullette.com and omegle.com. They are each an excellent example of what your children can be exposed to on the web. Both are very graphic.
- Images posted via social media sites, even on *Snapchat*, remain out there forever.
- Encourage your children to have more face-to-face relationships and encounters.
- Make your home kid and teen friendly and encourage hang-outs in your home.
- Talk to your child about appropriate use of the Internet and photo-sharing.
- Talk to them about being truthful on the Internet, and about how much should be shared online.
- The cognitive function of 'judgment' doesn't develop until the early 20s.

- Watch the movies *Catfish* (2010), *Bully* (2011), and *Cyberbully* (2011) with your teen.
- Have conversations with your children about cyber-bullying and the effects of it.

About the Experts

Dr. David Greenfield

Dr. Greenfield is widely acknowledged as one of the world's leading authorities on Internet and digital media technology behavior and abuse. In 1999 he wrote the book on Virtual Addiction and has successfully treated hundreds of people for it.

He has appeared numerous times on national news and interview programs, as well as in print. For over 20 years he has been giving public and business talks on the nature and risks of technology addiction and how to treat it. Learn more about Dr. Greenfield at www.drdavidgreenfield.com.

David Ryan Polgar

David is a Connecticut based writer, attorney, and educator who often speaks on the topics of information overload, tech balance, creativity, digital footprints, and the future of tech. He is a frequent contributor to national and international media outlets.

As a tech ethicist, he speaks and writes about the ethical, legal, sociological, and emotional issues surrounding our relationship to technology. He has been featured on SiriusXM, The Financial Times, HuffPost Live, Entrepreneur, FoxNews.com, and many more. He is the author of *Wisdom in the Age of Twitter*, a short guide to better thinking. Learn more about David at www.DavidRyanPolgar.com.

Bill Corbett

Interview 7:
Safe Driving Tips for Parents of Teens

Bill: Here is the second of two interviews I did with Tim Hollister, the AAA Club of Southern New England Traffic Safety Hero of the Year" in 2013. As the recipient of the U.S. Department of Transportation's "National Public Service Award" in 2010, the highest civilian honor for traffic safety, Mr. Hollister offered some detailed suggestions to parents of teenagers.

Thank you so much for being here to help educate parents about what they can do specifically to keep their teen drivers safe. I think the best way to start is to change their mindset about their teens and driving. What do you say?

Tim: I agree and maybe the place to start is with a tip that covers a lot of ground: don't put your own convenience ahead of your teen's safety. When your teen gets a license it is so convenient to use them as a new pickup and delivery service or your own new chauffeur. Up until now, you'd been getting up at the crack of dawn to drive your other children to school, but now you have someone to do that for you. There are so many places where it's easy to just let your teen take the keys and go when it's not safe for them to do so. So that's a real mindset change for a lot of parents.

When I do my presentations, a lot of people come up to me afterwards and say "Okay, I've read your blog and I've read your book; where do I start?" To help them, I've come up with a formula, **P.A.C.T.S–PACTS**. It represents the five biggest dangers in teen driving, and I tell parents, if you can get your arms around these five things, you'll be well on your way to raising a safe driver.

P is for passengers. Joy riding and passengers are the most dangerous situations for your teen.

A is for alcohol. Now, I'm not an expert in alcohol, but obviously alcohol and driving is a huge national problem and it's particularly a problem for teens.

C is for curfews—no night driving. We see a lot of crashes with teen drivers after 11 PM and midnight. Parents have to work with their teens because managing curfews ensures that they are off the road in accordance with state laws and this requires some planning. Help them develop their ability to judge what time they have to leave wherever they are, so they aren't rushing and driving too fast to get to wherever they need to be.

T is for texting. There must be zero tolerance for electronic devices, and by the way, that's not just cell phones. That includes the dashboard mounted interactive screens that are becoming so prevalent in cars.

S is for seat belt. Wearing a seat belt at all times should be a no brainer for every teen driver, and for every passenger of a teen driver.

Bill: One thing we talked about in my first interview with you is that the prefrontal cortex of the brain is not fully developed until the early 20's, and this is the part of the brain that gives our kids their ability to judge, think forward, and to have the ability to figure out "If I do this, then this is going to happen." Instead, their thinking is often consumed with the excitement of risk-taking. I want parents to understand that our kids aren't bad kids. It's just that cognitively, they are not yet adults and don't have the full capacity to think like an adult.

Tim: You're right, and no amount of teen driving experience is going to overcome that brain development issue.

Bill: Tim, you mentioned something else in our previous interview about the lack of hours of driving experience. Can you comment on that again?

Tim: Typically, teens in the United States get their license after 40 or 50 hours, but it really takes somewhere between 3 and 5 years to become a relatively safe driver. So the number of hours we require to get a license is nothing compared to the amount of experience needed to become a comfortable and competent driver. And this is another tip for parents; do not think that just because your son or daughter has taken driver's education classes and has passed the state's road and written test, that they are a safe driver. They are beginners at a very dangerous undertaking.

Bill: Your book, *Not So Fast,* is a great read for parents. One of the sections that I noticed in your book is about traffic tickets being teaching moments. Tell us a little bit about that.

Tim: You don't want the conversation with your teen when they come home with a ticket in their hand to start with them talking about how stupid law enforcement is, and how they didn't do anything wrong. You know how teens can be sometimes. If they have a ticket, then chances are, they did something wrong. But I think it's very important that parents do all they can to teach their teens to understand and respect law enforcement. When Massachusetts implemented its much stricter teen driver law a couple of years ago, there were news stories about parents going to court with their teens and yelling at the prosecutors. In my opinion, that was probably because the parents were about to lose a convenience, "I have of a teen driver and you're threatening to take that away from me." Parents went ballistic about that. But think about that for a moment; a parent yelling at a prosecutor with the teen standing right there to see that kind of behavior. Parents need to tell their teens, "You need to respect law enforcement because the law is there for a reason, and the people who enforce it are doing it for a very good reason—your own safety."

Bill: I'm guessing that some of that bad behavior on the part of the parent comes from them suffering from what's called the 'halo effect'—my child wouldn't do anything I wouldn't want him or her to do. Or "Why can't you just give him or her a break this one time because they're a new driver?"

Tim: Yes, I agree. When parents tell me that their kid is very responsible, I tell them that the key word in that sentence is 'kid'. They are just a kid.

Bill: Exactly. In another chapter you talk about the ceremony of keys. Tell us more about that.

Tim: I like to encourage parents to adapt the attitude of an air traffic controller—another chapter in the book. The car doesn't leave the drive way until you go over a safety checklist with your teen. One of the things you should say to your teen is, "I'm about to give you the keys because you are about to do something very dangerous." Make a big deal of turning over the keys each and every time your teen gets behind the wheel. I always say, "You wouldn't toss the keys to an airline pilot and say 'just be careful' so you shouldn't do that with a teen driver either." Make a big deal about turning over those car keys and go through your safety checklist every time, especially in the first year of driving.

Bill: Many teens probably resist it by saying something like, "Come on Mom, you don't trust me!" This resistance from the teen then causes parents to give up their position. I think that you're right, parents need to be persistent; they really need to make it formal. If you're putting them out there on the highway with tons of steel, safety should be an issue. Here's another chapter on negotiating and enforcing an agreement. I really like this one. Tell us more.

Tim: When it comes to driving, parent/teen agreements are an essential and much underutilized tool. This is something to negotiate; you don't just tell them. You negotiate with your teen about what the rules are, and what the consequences are if the rules are broken. You do this when you and your teen are calm, not when they come home all flustered because they got a ticket. I did about two years of research and there's hundreds and hundreds of models for teen driver agreements out there. I took what I thought were the best elements and included a national model of a teen driving agreement in my book.

Connecticut has actually adopted its own model, which was based somewhat on mine, so I was very gratified by that. Their number one priority is establishing what the risks are and setting clear rules. I see so many agreements from national organizations where the rules just aren't very clear. Some agreements state that if the teen violates the law, they may lose privileges. What does that mean? Using a teen driver's agreement with your teen driver is a commitment to safety and it's important that this be a collaborative process. It's unfortunate that it's such an underutilized tool.

Bill: You also have a chapter about when teens should really start driving.

Tim: Yes, there's the issue of the legal age versus the age of responsibility and so maybe, turn that around. An important piece of advice for parents is–don't push a teen who is not ready to drive, to do so. Don't think that you're going to get your teen to grow up any faster by driving; that's exactly the wrong way to push their progress. Parents have to use their judgment to decide if their teen has the emotional maturity required to operate a motor vehicle safely. We talked earlier about judgment and how the teen brain isn't developed until the early twenties. Also, not every kid is the same, and you need to make that assessment. Some teens just aren't ready to drive even though the law says they can get their learners permit.

Bill: Let's talk about texting and electronic devices.

Tim: Texting is driving blind folded. You're taking your hands off the wheel, your eyes off the road, and you're mind off the situation. I advocate a zero tolerance policy for parents by which I mean the cell phone goes in the glove box before the ignition is turned on, and it stays there until the ignition is turned off. I am not a fan of these apps where the phone is in the cradle and it's supposed to send an electronic message - "I'm driving I'll call you later." It's probably better than nothing, but if the phone is in the cradle, the temptation to pick it up is almost overwhelming.

What we're talking about here is one side of the brain overwhelming the other. If you think about the fact that texting makes a crash 23 times more likely than normal driving, which is already dangerous for a teen, it's a crash and injury waiting to happen. And parents have to be role models. I tell parents that if you've got one of those interactive screens in your car and you're pushing the buttons and you're reading restaurant reviews or updating your Facebook page while you're driving, you're going to have a hard time telling your teen not to text when you are doing something just as bad.

Bill: Today's teenagers are tethered to their texting devices, feeling compelled to constantly check for new texts or social media updates from their friends. It's a huge distraction to whatever they're doing at the moment. It becomes too difficult to not touch that electronic device while they're in the car.

Tim: Yes; teens need to feel connected and all of those devices have a very powerful magnetic force.

Bill: Thank you so much for taking time out for this interview Tim. I know that many parents are grateful for the work you've done on this matter, including myself as the stepdad to a teenage girl. You've turned your personal tragedy into something that is going to save thousands of lives. There cannot be too much education on the topic of helping parents keep their teen drivers safe and alive. I wish you all the best.

SUMMARY

- Don't put your own convenience ahead of your teen's safety.
- P is for Passengers - Do not allow your teen to go joy riding (no destination in mind) with passengers.
- A is for Alcohol - Do not allow your teen to drive while drinking alcohol.
- C is for Curfew - Curfews must be adhered to. Help your teen driver to plan ahead so they aren't rushing.
- T is for Texting - There must be zero tolerance for texting while driving.
- S is for Seatbelts - Seatbelts must be worn by everyone in the car.
- Taking driver's education classes and successfully passing the exams doesn't instantly turn your teen into a safe driver.
- Teach your teen driver to respect the law and law enforcement personnel.
- Avoid thinking that your teen would never do anything wrong.
- The car doesn't leave the driveway until a safety check is completed.

- Make a big deal out of turning over the keys to your teen driver.
- Negotiate a written agreement with your teen driver that includes clear consequences.
- Don't push a teen to drive if he or she isn't ready to drive.
- Do not allow teens to text or be distracted by other devices while driving, and set a good example with your own driving habits.
- Teach them to place their phone in the glove box before driving away.

About the Expert

Tim Hollister

Mr. Hollister has become a national authority and spokesperson for safer teen driving since losing his 17 year old son Reid in a car crash in 2006. After serving on a Connecticut task force in 2007 that overhauled the state's teen driver laws, in 2009 Tim launched "From Reid's Dad," a national blog for parents of teen drivers, that now attracts more than 20,000 visitors per month and is relied upon by traffic safety organizations, driving schools, and parents throughout the country. Tim has appeared on national and regional programs such as "Raising America" on HLN and "Mr. Dad."

In 2013, Tim's book *Not So Fast: Parenting Your Teen Through the Dangers of Driving* was released by the Chicago Review Press. Publishers Weekly has called the book "A concise, practical and potentially life-saving book that should be required reading for every parent before their teen gets behind the wheel." Tim was named the AAA Club of Southern New England's Traffic Safety Hero of the Year in 2013, and in 2010 he received the U.S. Department of Transportation's National Public Service Award, the nation's highest civilian honor for traffic safety. Tim is an environmental attorney and lives in Bloomfield, CT.

Interview 8:
Breaking Through to Tough Teens

Bill: If you live or work with teenagers you probably know firsthand how difficult it can be to connect with them sometimes. They can be impulsive, secretive, and moody. Someone once said that raising teenagers is like trying to nail jello to a tree. But one man has taken on this challenge seriously. I have the privilege of interviewing Mr. Dan Blanchard, an author and speaker on motivating teens. He's also a school teacher in one Connecticut's largest inner-city high schools. He's the author of' the book, *Granddaddy's Secrets*, a teen leadership book series that defines the importance of one generation passing wisdom to the next. Mr. Blanchard is a former two time junior Olympian wrestler and has completed 12 years of college, earning seven degrees in the field of education.

You work in the school system Dan, so you're probably someone who interacts with teenagers living in probably some of the toughest situations. I would assume you can only guess about what kinds of situations, neighborhoods, or families they come from, and you have to use that background information in your teaching. Tell us a little bit more about the background that you have that enables you to understand teens.

Dan: I have been an inner-city school teacher for about 20 years now and I have written a couple teen literature books and have been a coach in different sports: wrestling and football and some power lifting. So I've spent a lot of time with teens through their public education, with sports, through the coaching, and I also have 5 kids of my own now, so I've definitely spent a lot of time around kids. I have to admit, it's never easy... but it's doable, it really is.

Bill: Are any of your kids teens yet?

Dan: No, but they certainly act like they are. My oldest is 12 and believe it or not, she's pretty much the easiest one. It's the next one, the 9 year old, that's a little more challenging. He wants to be grown up overnight and the man of the house, something I see quite frequently in the inner-city when dealing with teen boys. Some of them unfortunately don't have father figures, so from an early age they're the man of the house. They could be like 5, 6, 7, or 8 years old and are the man of the house and then when you get them as a teenager, they've been the man of the house for a while. When someone tells them what to do, they look at you like you're crazy. They say something like "I'm the man of the house, so you're not going to tell me what to do." Then the adult starts butting heads with them. This is probably quite frequent in all places, but particularly the inner-city.

Bill: You've got a couple of books out, you're working on a few more, and based on our earlier conversation, you told me that it's all about passing wisdom down from generation to generation. I agree with you. I think it's so important but unfortunately, with parents being so busy, I think we've lost that art and wisdom of storytelling. I know that when I was a kid, I'd listen to my grandparent's stories, but I don't think that happens much anymore.

Dan: No it doesn't, and I think one of the reasons why it doesn't happen is because it takes time to tell a good story. It takes a lot more time than just saying to someone, "Read this paragraph and answer this question." And it seems like today's trend in education—and society, is that everybody is so busy everywhere, that they're trying to maximize the impact, so we end up trying to shove information down people's throats and then say "Spit it back at me. Did you get it? Do you know it? And do you have it memorized yet?" It's tough to perform at that level because what happens is they don't get time for it to sink in, so it's hard to just spit stuff back and act like you really got it.

All that happens is that kids just spit it back and they didn't really get it. Whereas with the story, you can listen to a story and you can get it on one level but then maybe later on, when you're lying in bed that night trying to fall asleep, its sinking in on a different level. Maybe a couple years later it will be sinking in much deeper on another different level, this takes time. We're in such a 'hurry up' society today that unfortunately, storytelling is a lost art. It's not so easy to measure the results of a story; it's much easier to measure 2+2=4.

Bill: You're so right, that we've lost the art of storytelling. Entertainment back then (in our grandparent's time) was storytelling, but now we've got video and movies and computers and the internet, and I think that has replaced a lot of the time that was used to pass down wisdom through storytelling.

Dan: Adults today are going to have to be really good at storytelling if we want to keep our teens' attention, or pretty much anyone's attention, exactly for the reasons you are saying. You're now competing with a whole array of things and its tough, but it's worth the effort.

Bill: So you obviously have a lot of expertise dealing with teens. Parents who are reading this can benefit greatly from what you have to say. So what advice do you have for adults on how to better gain the attention of teens?

Dan: There's no one easy way to do it. I've had parents come to me in parent teacher conferences or pull me aside to talk. I've seen the frustration in their faces for years and years. They say things like, "My kid won't listen to me. I tell my kid something and he does the opposite. It goes in one ear and comes out the other." So one of the things I try to tell them is to just relax. I tell them that believe it or not, they're getting it. They're hearing you; their just acting like they're not hearing you.

Therefore, the worst thing the parent could do is to give up and worse, go into a combat mode. You can't go into 'combative mode' with your teen; you have to stay in the 'love mode.' You have to just keep giving them your messages over and over again, calmly, even though maybe it feels like it's been a million times that you've given them that same message. Do your best to keep giving it to them with warmth and love and know that at some point, they're going to say, "Remember when you said 'such and such'?" I can't count how many times I've been a witness to that.

Bill: As a parenting expert, I learned that when our kids get into the adolescent years, they actually develop an allergy to their parents. What happens is that they have to shed their 'baby image' to enable them to progress to the next level of young adulthood. And who is attached to that baby image? The parents are, and it's the parents that they appear to be rejecting. That allergy or rejection makes it appear as if they don't want to be with their parents. Part of that rejection is the teen seeing their parents as dumb and stupid. But what about school; how do we get teens to engage better in school? From your perspective... you're the teacher talking to parents, what would you say?

Dan: One thing I tell them is that they've got to have a set homework time at home, and it's not negotiable. Whether it's right after the teen gets off the bus or following an after-school activity such as a sport, doing homework should come first, then they can get on their electronics or go and play. There has to be a set homework time that's non-negotiable. And of course, they're going to fight with the parent and say something like "I left my book in school," "I didn't have any homework," or "The teacher gave me homework but I finished it real quick, it was easy." So if they give you all these reasons as to why they don't have homework, be ready to give them your own assignment to fill that homework time. Have books and magazines ready for them to read and then write a summary on. You can say to them, "If you're not going to do your teacher's homework, then you're going to do mine."

Keep giving them that homework hour of extra reading and then sooner or later, if they are indeed blowing off their teacher's homework, they're likely to say to themselves, "My mom and dad are making me do homework, so I might as well just do the homework that the teacher gave to me." And let's say that they really ARE doing the official homework during other classes or on the bus, then an extra hour of reading is only going to help them. You're actually doing them a favor.

Bill: Excellent advice Dan. I really agree with you on that. In fact, I'm always advising parents to set the homework time in stone and make sure that it happens. Now of course it's difficult at times if the child has after-school activities or if there are family activities after school. But you must do all that you can to make sure that homework time happens every night, Sunday through Thursday. I also tell parents that their job during homework time is to eliminate the distractions. It's their job to get the kids to check-in cell phones, tablets, computers, and other hand-held devices during that time.

The primary reason that something must be worked on during homework time every weekday is to carve out and preserve that time so that it happens and never disappears. What would stop a teenager from telling their parent that they had no homework on a day when their assignments were really difficult? Imagine them coming home and having to choose between completing a tough assignment or playing with their Xbox when all they really have to do is lie to the parent about having homework. Then, later that evening, the teen announces that he forgot he had homework to do. If parents implement and stand behind this mandatory guideline - no internet or electronic entertainment during the first few hours immediately following school, their teens are less likely to allow distractions to keep them from working on homework.

Bill: Dan, how were you able to complete seven degrees?

Dan: Believe it or not, I was never a good student. I was a typical C student in high school and then went into the service. When I got out, I convinced myself that it was time to go to school and to focus. I used some of that energy and discipline that I got from previous sports and the military, and I focused on college. I got good grades for my work on the first degree and that just fed into getting another degree. I got another degree, and then another degree, and the good grades just kept that momentum going. I couldn't seem to stop; I just kept going.

Bill: Do you have any advice for teachers who teach in high schools? What about the teachers who are burned out because they're not having as much success as you have had? What would you say to those teachers?

Dan: I would say "It's not your fault that you're burned out because teaching is one of the most demanding jobs out there." People don't realize how demanding it really is. I'd also say, if teaching tough kids in high school has changed your paradigm and the way you are looking at your class, it's not going to magically change. Your tough students aren't going to instantly do the things you want them too. But if you reach out to them with kindness and work hard at developing a relationship with them—no matter what they do or how they act, you will begin to break through to them. If you send little post cards and notes home with them—no matter what they do, you're going to put yourself in better spirits and your students are going to take notice. In the end they are going to want to be around you and want to start working harder for you. It won't happen overnight, but at some point, they're likely to look at you differently and say to themselves, "I've been pushing this teacher's buttons and he/she is still there... in my corner." The next thing you'll notice is that they'll start going through brick walls for you. So be as kind as you can be, and no matter what happens, always put that smile on your face and build that relationship and then you'll see. You'll actually start feeling better inside regardless of what you're facing."

Bill: That reminds me of a quote from author John C. Maxwell who said "People don't care how much you know, until they know how much you care." That goes right along with what you're saying. It applies to kids, parenting, and school.

Dan: Very true.

Bill: I've often told teachers that children and teens are affected by adult emotional chaos. If a teacher walks into the classroom stressed out, that stress is transferred to each of the kids in that classroom, making both teaching and learning difficult. Dan, you've got a really difficult job and I'm glad you're doing what you're doing. We need more teachers like you who are really striving to make a difference in teenagers in school. Please keep doing what you're doing and thanks for agreeing to this interview.

SUMMARY:

- Pass wisdom on to your kids and teens through storytelling.
- Your teens must reject you as part of their normal development; don't take it personally.
- Continue conveying your messages to your teen, even if they don't seem to be listening.
- Convey those messages with calmness and love; avoid getting combative with them.
- Establish a nonnegotiable homework time each day, Sunday - Thursday PM.
- Be ready to give them homework if they rarely seem to come home with any; have them read a book or magazine article and write a review.
- Parents should remove distractions (such as the Internet) during homework time.
- Use kindness and encouragement with tough teens. Write them encouraging notes.

- Teens need to know how much you care, even though they act like they don't.

About the Expert

Dan Blanchard

Dan Blanchard has done his homework. He's been an inner-city school teacher and athletic coach for 20 years and has a passion for teaching, inspiring, and working with teens. Dan is the author of the book *Feeling Lucky?* and is an award winning author, speaker, and educator who shares real-life lessons and inspiring stories with audiences of teens, adults, educators, and sometimes a mixture of all three. His goal is to positively influence the way we think about what is possible, regardless of how old we are. Visit his website: GranddaddysSecrets.com.

Interview 9:

Setting Teen Boys Up For Success

Bill: Like many parents, I hoped my son would get through adolescence safely and make it to his young adult years with great success. I got my wish and I'm enjoying watching him live a very productive adult life. But getting that to happen wasn't all just luck, there are many things that parents can do to help their boys, ages 10-18, reach their full potential. Here is my interview of two Dads who have some advice to share with us on this topic.

Tommy Maloney is a dad and a hockey coach who teaches parenting classes with his wife Annie in Denver, Colorado. He is the author of the book *25 Tips for Divorced Dads: How to Create Special Memories and Grow Your Bonds with Your Children*. Jeff

Londraville has a master's degree in education with a concentration in Counseling Psychology from Cambridge College in Boston. He is the author of the book *The Filter*, a book that teaches young people how to realize their full potential by sifting through all the events, both positive and negative, that affect their lives.

It's not easy for parents to figure out how to get their kids to reach their full potential, but let me ask you, what do you think stops kids? Are there barriers that get in the way?

Jeff: That's exactly why I wrote the book *The Filter*. In it, I wrote about some of those things that do get in the way. So many books directed toward teenagers tell them about success. They prescribe doing this and doing that, but I've not seen a lot of evidence that teens are implementing what they read. They don't really like being told that they should do this or do that.

Adults working with, or raising teen boys will be more successful connecting with them if they empathize with them first. Help them see that the adult understands what they are going through. Sometimes it requires adult caregivers to remember what it was like to be a teenager. We're so quick to want them to reach their full potential, but we don't always know how to get to the blocks that get in their way. We must help unclog the negativity of whatever is preventing them from doing better. We have to sort of guide them to get 'unstuck' first.

Tommy: I believe that Einstein once stated that one of the worst things people can do is crush creativity in others, especially children. Some parents see their children acting like children and don't see that as just being creative. An example of that creativity is what my son and his *bonus* sister have been doing together. They created not one, but two businesses. As parents, we're educating and encouraging them to keep at it, and not to be afraid to fail. I think a lot of times, kids end up being afraid to fail. In a way, without realizing it, we end up saying to them, "I failed and it wasn't fun, so I don't want you to fail. Therefore, don't do it."

Bill: Tommy, I have to ask you what a *bonus* sister is.

Tommy: I've never understood what a '*step*' is; stepsister, stepbrother, stepdad, etc. Years ago I heard the term BONUS, so I started calling my stepdad my Bonus Dad, because to me, it's a bonus to have him in my life. I also think it's a bonus for me to have my wife's two daughters in my life and my son's life. Therefore, I have two bonus daughters and my son has two bonus sisters. Many years ago, I remember him saying, "I wish I had a sister." Now he has two!

I wrote my book from the aspect of being a divorced dad and thinking "I'm not in that house anymore. How do I create a bond with my son without being there?" I encourage dads to stay connected and stay bonded with their kids even after the divorce. I encourage them not to become an absent dad. You must get out and be with your kids. And if your kids live in a separate state, you're going to have to get creative about planning your vacation time so you can connect with your kids. Staying connected means using whatever means you have to keep that connection. For example, using Skype on the computer and calling them on the telephone. I like to send my son postcards, especially when I travel for my job: I send him post cards from different cities. It's another way of keeping that connection.

Bill: Great ideas Tommy. It's so important to make our connection with our kids a top priority, especially when we don't live with our kids anymore. Jeff, your book is all about filtering out the negative aspects of the world for our kids, right? Tell us a little more about it.

Jeff: Right. In it I wrote about the things that prevent someone from developing high self-esteem and understanding the difference between both good and bad role models. And taking individual responsibility is something that seems to be slipping away. My book offers suggestions on how to help kids to not only become more responsible for their actions, but also to take action on things they see around them. We need to get back to the whole, *it takes a village to raise a child* mindset and at the same time, explore how to remove the negativity around us that kills creativity.

Bill: There does seem to be a lack of individual responsibility in the world today. I'd like the two of you to offer some tips to parents and grandparents, and anyone who lives or cares for teen boys, on how adults can get the message to kids that they've got potential and to go out and make use of it. What can you offer?

Tommy: Here's a simple tip that's in my book. It's sad that we have to make this a tip to remind parents, but I just don't see enough of it in the world. It's: *tell your kids everyday that you love them*. It seems like such a no-brainer, but I think some parents find it incredibly difficult to actually do. I think that if our kids confidently know that their parents love them, even when they're misbehaving or goofing off, I think it helps shape and form their self-esteem. Like Jeff said about it being in his book, we must help our kids grow their self-esteem with small things we can do every day.

Jeff: I agree and want to offer: communicating with your kids. I think that every day we must take ordinary, everyday topics and use them to open up the lines of communications with our kids. Parents are so busy trying to keep up with everything that communicating with their kids seems to take a back seat. We can't wait for something bad to happen with our kids, with ourselves, or something in the family, to start talking to them.

When we establish strong lines of communication with our kids, and at the same time, avoid yelling, screaming, and punishing, it encourages our kids to think to themselves, "I can go to my mom or my dad about anything, and that feels great." We want them to know that we're there, available, and ready to listen. It all starts with a basic conversation. They begin to feel they can trust us and that opens up the door to any type of dialogue. It's within this dialogue that you can slip in the little questions such as, "So… how's school going?" or "Is anything bothering you?" It's all about creating a warm and welcoming atmosphere for your children to WANT to talk to you. It's all about creating that open line of basic conversation before the major conversations need to happen, and not WHEN something has to be discussed.

Bill: Great point Jeff. You're talking about setting up and creating an environment that's conducive for them to share. It's also helpful for parents to learn how to ask open-ended questions that invite the kind of dialogue we're talking about.

Tommy: It seems that society in some ways, has defined asking for help as a sign of weakness. This is especially true when it comes to boys. And feelings is another area where boys aren't supposed to express emotions; they're supposed to suppress them. Boys are supposed to be tough and suck it up. It seems as if society has done a number on young men. This is even more of a reason why parents need to develop those lines of communication. They're so vital for kids who are seeking help, guidance, and answers to questions that come up in their mind every day.

Bill: Tommy, you speak at conferences on being a divorced dad, but do you also speak on boys and emotion?

Tommy: I do. One of the things that Jeff mentioned earlier about opening up the lines of communication really resonated with me. I remarried last year and during the wedding I noticed that my 10-year-old son Connor was crying. My initial reaction was "Hold on here... why are you crying... I'm in the middle of getting married," and then I started to cry as well. I really wanted to stop everything and attend to his emotions, but I couldn't. To your point Jeff, I waited until sometime after the wedding and struck up a conversation with him as a normal dialogue.

Then I found the right time to slip in the question, "What was the problem at the wedding? You looked like you were sad." He then simply said, "I wasn't, I was happy." I think he learned that it was OK to cry at that moment and to not hold it in. As a boy, I had gotten the message that I'm supposed to know everything and I shouldn't cry. I've got great guy friends and we hug. We don't do the bro handshake thing like most men do. I want my son to see that, and I hope it helps him understand his own feelings too.

Bill: Jeff, Tommy, thank you both for being available for this interview and for sharing all that you did. I hope parents seeing or reading this interview will be encouraged to let their boys feel their own emotions and communicate openly with their parents.

SUMMARY
- Teenage boys first need to know that you care about them before they will care about what you can teach them.
- Dads connecting with teen boys should do their best to remember

what it was like when they themselves were teenagers.

- Encourage creativity in your teen boys and avoid the urge to protect them from failure.
- When they fail, wait for the emotion to subside and then encourage them to talk about what happened.
- Divorced dads living away from their sons should connect with them often.
- Divorced dads can connect using Skype, the telephone, and sending post cards or letters.
- Don't become an absent dad. Stay in your children's lives in any way you can.
- Emphasize or introduce more positive role models to your children.
- Tell your kids you love them every day.
- Have regular dialogues with your teenage boys, especially where there is nothing urgent to discuss.

- Let your boys know that asking for help is a sign of strength, not weakness.
- Invite your teen boys to share their feelings regularly.
- Let your teenage boys see you expressing your emotions so they know it's an OK thing to do.

About the Experts

Tommy Maloney

He's a dad, "bonus dad", and author of the book *25 Tips for Divorced Dads: How to create special memories and grow your bonds with your children*. Tommy speaks on stages to divorced fathers nationally in hopes of inspiring them to stay connected to their children. Mr. Maloney is happily married and makes his home near Boulder, CO. You can learn more about him at tommymaloneyinternational.com

Jeff Londraville, M.Ed

With a Master's Degree in Education with a concentration in Counseling Psychology from Cambridge College in Boston, Jeff is the author of the book *The Filter: Unclogging the Negativity that is Preventing You From Having a Wonderful Life*, a book for teenagers and adults. He's is the director for new school development for Sabis Educational Services.

Bill Corbett

Interview 10:
Raising Teen Boys

Bill: I've gathered a panel of experts on raising teen boys, with the intention of getting them to help me come up with tips for raising teenage boys with great success. Dr.Clint Steel is the founder of the *Pay it Forward One Million Times* project based in Portland, Maine. Jim Bouchard is a professional speaker and author of the book *Think Like A Black Belt* and also from Portland Maine. Tommy Maloney is a Dad, a parent educator, the author of the book *25 Tips for Divorced Dads*, and lives in Denver, Colorado. Last but not least, Jeff Londraville is an educator and author of the book *The Filter* and lives near Springfield, Massachusetts.

I've put together a list of questions and statements from parents of teenagers and want to pass them by you all to see if you have any wisdom to offer up. Let's get started with the first one regarding testosterone surges that boys experience. It's been said that these surges blunt their fear, making them more susceptible to dangerous behaviors and even increases anger through competition.

Tommy: As a hockey coach and a father of a son who plays hockey, one of the things that I stress is that sports for boys must be fun. I've seen too much bad coaching that drives boys to a point of getting angry and feeling hatred toward their opponents. These coaches don't help at all, demanding that "We have to win... We have to win every single game, and if we don't win, you guys are going to do laps." The fear of losing turns to threats and that builds up their anger. So I'm not sure how it's all related to the testosterone surges, but coaches must teach their teens the fundamentals of the sport and stress to them to also go out and have fun.

Jeff: I agree and would like to add that every moment is a teaching moment. It's also how you speak to the kids about the teaching moment. If you always come across as if you're preaching to or lecturing a teenager or any child, it becomes a little monotonous and they may not actually be taking in what you're saying. But if you use the right words and tone, you can actually influence how a child thinks and behaves. Every time I put my 8-year-old daughter to sleep I say to her, "Honey, sleep good and wake up better." I want her to rest easy and get a good night's sleep. She does this because we talk about what happened throughout the day and together we process her experiences.

Bill: I had the opportunity to interview Dr. Anthony Wolf recently. He's the author of the book *Get Out Of My Life: But First Can You Drive Me and Cheryl to the Mall*. It's a great book on now to understand adolescents better. One of the things that I learned in that interview was some of the reasoning behind why raising teenagers better is like trying to give a cat a bath. In order for them to grow toward young adulthood, they must first rid themselves of the image that they were once a baby. And because their parents are attached to the baby image, they actually begin to reject their parents to some extent. Dr. Wolf humorously said they become allergic to their parents. This presents some behavior issues at home for parents.

He also pointed out some differences between the two genders during this development period that I want to share with you. He said that girls generally tend to separate themselves from their parents by declaring their independence, moment by moment, and sometimes in your face. That is, they love to argue and verbally declare their independence. But boys are a little different. Boys tend to separate themselves from their parents physically. They begin to spend more time in their rooms with the doors closed and they begin to reject the physical affection, especially when they become aware of the fact that their mother is a girl. It can be a bit awkward for them when Mom reaches out for hugs and kisses.

Jeff: I always tell teenagers that their words, actions, and even how they dress, actually teaches others how to treat them. Everywhere you go, whether it's at school or at home, you always have more control than you think you do. Teenagers don't think they have control as they walk the bridge from childhood to adulthood, but they actually do. Parents on the other hand are experiencing their own dilemma. Metaphorically speaking, they are trying to hold their young teenager's hand through it all and aren't sure when to let go. In a sense, they're afraid their kids will fall off of the bridge and they don't know when to let go.

It's truly important that we adults stress to our young people that everything they do teaches others how to treat them. As I said, they have more control then they may realize. Now of course, I tell them that people will be unfair to you at times but you still have more control than you think you do. This is so important for teens to understand because too many of them think everyone is out to get them, or that others are constantly telling them what to do.

Jim: And related to feeling that others are out to get them, I want to bring up the topic of parents spying on their kids and monitoring their activities. I tell the teens in the school system I work with that when your parents are monitoring you, it's actually an act of caring and I think that's what needs to be communicated. The teen is likely to push back and say something like, "Why are you in my face all the time, don't you trust me?" That deserves the response from the parent, "It's not that I don't trust you, but it's my job to keep you safe."

Bill: Some parents believe that we should give our teens lots of privacy and we shouldn't monitor them. I take the stance that we must monitor them so we know who they are in contact with. I let my kids know that I'm monitoring them as well. Teenagers have very poor judgment. The prefrontal cortex or the front of the brain isn't fully developed until the early 20s and it's that part of the teenage brain that provides judgment and planning.

Jim: In my experience, I've found that teens don't like it when parents try to be their teenager's friend by dressing like them and wanting to hang out with them and their friends. They really don't like it when Mom is wearing teen clothes and Dad is acting like he's a member of the baseball team. If we want kids to develop into responsible adults, we have to model that behavior for them. We must lead by example? Being playful is fine some of the time, but the rest of the time, it's up to the parents to demonstrate what being an adult looks like.

Dr. Steele: I agree with what Jeff said earlier. We must show that every experience is a lesson for them to learn, whether it's a positive one or a negative one. With all that they're learning, it's so important for adults to keep tabs on the teens in their lives. Whether you're a parent or a teacher, we have to stay in touch to monitor them to some extent. They don't yet have the cognitive capacity to manage themselves completely. Yes, it's part of a boy's experience of becoming a man to want to distance himself from his parents and want more freedom and privacy, but they are in a learning mode and need some supervision.

Jim: And things might have turned out differently for some of us if our parents had kept better tabs on us.

Tommy: How powerful and yet simple it is to teach a kid one little life lesson at a time. That little nugget of knowledge is huge and will impact him or her for a lifetime. At coffee shops, I've seen a person in line pay for their drink and also buy one for the person behind them. I love doing that and the people at the coffee place say thank you because they know how the next person in line is likely to do it for the person in back of them, and so on and so on. We parents need to be thinking about paying it forward ourselves. When our kids see us at our worst, they're going to emulate what they see. But we have the power to have them see us in our best moments, and that's what we want them to emulate more. We end up passing on a legacy.

Jim: How about just being polite? I mean that's a huge lesson that gets easily lost. You were saying something about this earlier Dr. Steel, that it's the smallest examples. I've seen kids walk by the door and not even say hello or not even acknowledge you. I always ask my kids in the martial arts program, what are the two most important words in martial arts. The answer is *paying attention* and if we pay attention to the world around us, we see much less ugliness and much more beauty. But we have to teach kids that they don't automatically know this. We have to educate them.

Bill: Jim, you made a remark earlier about kids' rejection of their parents who are trying to be like them and dress like them. One day my stepdaughter, or bonus daughter, and I were together and I used a word or phrase that she usually says. To that she said, "Don't, just don't." It was almost as if her generation owned that phrase and adults shouldn't be using it.

In closing, I'd like to say thank you to each of you for all the time and energy you spend helping teenagers. Every bit of it makes a difference.

SUMMARY
- Make sports fun and a positive learning experience.
- Avoid making winning a greater importance over teamwork and fun.
- Every moment with a child is a teaching moment that will stay with them forever.
- Avoid preaching or lecturing to a teenager.

- It is psychologically normal for a teenager to reject his or her parents.
- Teenagers become 'allergic' to their parents.
- Boys and girls tend to separate themselves from their parents in different ways.
- Girls distance themselves by arguing and declaring their independence verbally.
- Boys distance themselves by spending more time alone in their room.
- Boys sometimes distance themselves from their mothers when they realize she's a girl.
- A teenager's words, actions, and how they dress determine how others will treat them.
- Monitor your kids to keep them safe from predators.
- The judgment ability of teens is critically low.
- Don't act or dress like your teen; allow them to have their own identity.

- Set a good example for your teens on what an adult looks and acts like.
- Help your teen see that every experience, good and bad, are learning experiences.
- Teach your teens to pay good deeds and kindness forward without rewards.
- Show them the importance of paying attention to the world around them.
- Demonstrate etiquette and polite behavior toward others.

About the Experts

(From left to right: Bill Corbett, Dr. Clint Steele, Tommy Maloney, Jeff Londraville, and Jim Bouchard)

Dr. Clint Steele began mentoring and working with youth as an 18-year-old All-American high school football player. He received his doctorate at the age of 23 and then spent the next 15 years building a multi-location chiropractic practice near Portland, ME. Today, Dr. Steele is an entrepreneur and runs multiple organizations, including the inspirational *PAY IT FORWARD x1 MILLION*.

Tommy Maloney is a dad, a "bonus dad", and author of the book *25 Tips for Divorced Dads: How to create special memories and grow your bonds with your children.* He speaks on stages to divorced fathers nationally in hopes of inspiring them to stay connected to their children. Mr. Maloney is happily married and makes his home near Boulder, CO. You can learn more about him at http://tommymaloneyinternational.com

Jeff Londraville has a Master's Degree in Education with a concentration in Counseling Psychology from Cambridge College in Boston and is the author of the book *The Filter: Unclogging the Negativity that is Preventing You From Having a Wonderful Life*, a book for teenagers and adults. Jeff is the director for new school development for Sabis Educational Services. You can contact Jeff through LinkedIn by CLICKING THIS LINK.

Jim Bouchard increases engagement and productivity, and develops leadership at all levels of your organization- by teaching your people how to THINK Like a BLACK BELT. As a speaker, corporate trainer and author of the Amazon bestseller, *Think Like a Black Belt*, Jim tours nationally presenting his philosophy of Black Belt Mindset for corporate and conference audiences. He's a regular guest on TV and radio programs across the country and internationally. For more information, visit ThatBlackBeltGuy.com.

Bill Corbett

About the Author

Bill Corbett, CPE

Bill is a national parent educator and author of numerous parenting books. He is the author of the Parent Education Program *LOVE, LIMITS, & LESSONS.* Bill has a degree in clinical psychology and is an on-air contributor to ABC and NBC networks on matters of parenting, family, and child behavior. He provides parent coaching and keynote presentations to parent and professional audiences across the country. Bill is a father of three grown children, a grandfather of two, and a stepdad to three.

You can learn more about his work at www.CooperativeKids.com and www.BillCorbett.com.

The Following Additional Products for Parents by Bill Corbett can be Found at: CooperativeKids.vpweb.com

Love, Limits & Lessons: A Parent's Guide to Raising Cooperative Kids
An easy-to-read guide that offers solid common sense solutions for raising capable and cooperative kids in today's fast-paced world. Designed with the quick reference approach in mind, this book will allow you to turn immediately to the situations you find yourself faced with most often.

Get Out of My Life!: A Live Recorded Audio Program for Parents of Teenagers
Download this audio recording and listen to an entertaining audio presentation that will have you laughing at parents and teens alike as Bill Corbett lays out the irrefutable issues with raising teens. In this one hour and 20 minute audio recorded in front of a

live audience, Bill explains what it takes to become a successful parent with the modern-day teenager.

A Live Presentation of Love, Limits & Lessons Audio Download

Download this recording and enjoy a presentation of Bill Corbett's high energy and humorous presentation of his Love, Limits, & Lessons seminar to a live audience. Get ready to be entertained and educated on rebuilding the caregiver's discipline toolbox with tools needed for today's challenging child.

Another Serving of a Live Presentation of Love, Limits & Lessons Audio Download

In this NEW live audio recording, Bill challenges a room full of parents by introducing them to the 10 common problems that most parents face. He offers solutions to these problems along with strategies for managing them on a daily basis. Get ready, once again, to be entertained and educated on rebuilding the caregiver's discipline toolbox with techniques needed for today's challenging child.

The Expert's Guide to Teenagers

Made in the USA
Middletown, DE
21 February 2016